Crumbled Not Broken: Embracing the Mess in Healing and Baking

Dayna Altman
A project of Bake it Till You Make it LLC

Dedication

Dedicated to those who have always wondered if they are broken. The truth is, no matter what you have been through and how damaged you may feel, you have always been complete.

You, alone, are more than enough.

Acknowledgments

A special thanks to Jason Taglieri, no Bake it Till You Make it book is complete without your design, set up and/or expertise---your willingness to believe in me and bring my work into the world, has changed my life.

To all the Bake it Till You Make it community members: Gabby Alvarez, Mekkailah Chourb, Allee DeFronzo, Iwinosa Foster-Efosa, Melody Gregory, Beth Hobbs, Jason Taglieri and Jenna Williams, who illustrated these poems, thank you for giving your time and creativity to this project, you inspire me! It means more than I can express!

To my husband, Sam, who has never doubted my "wholeness".

To my therapists (Dena, Kelly, and Cathy): thank you for letting me tell our stories through poetry. My unique relationships with each of you have helped me lay the foundation that has allowed me to soar.

To you, thank you for going on this journey with me.

To me, thank you for believing in yourself enough to take it.

Table of Contents

I. A Beautiful Mess: The Everything But The Kitchen Sink Cookie

1. The "S" Word	2
2. 1AM	3
3. Limelight	4
4. Emetophobia	5
5. Public Speaker	6
6. Depression is a heavy hitter	7
7. Container	8
8. One	10
9. Distraction	11
10. Rx	12
11. Social Anxiety	13
12. Friend?	14
13. Depression	15
14. Joy	16
15. Death Anxiety	17
16. Dominos	18
17. Things that Feel like a hug	19

II. The Complexities Of Living In Diet Culture: The Sugar Cookie

1. Hunger	21
2. Perfect	22
3. 100 Things I would rather discuss than your diet	23
4. Preoccupation	26
5. Dad's Dilemma	27
6. Intersection	28
7. Finally some relief	29
8. Pedestal	30
9. Note to Self	32
10. Bride	33
11. Pain	35
12. 34 Constitution	36
13. Up All Night	37
14. Things that feel like Heartbreak	38

III. A Vulnerable Life Shouldn't Be Rare:
The Oatmeal Chocolate Chip Cookie

1. I Know	*40*
2. TMS	*41*
3. Sabotage	*42*
4. I miss my big feelings	*43*
5. This life	*45*
6. Ghost	*47*
7. Too Short	*48*
8. Present	*50*
9. Loved	*51*
10. Christmas Eve-Eve	*52*
11. Stay	*54*
12. Perfectionist	*55*
13. Painful Truth	*56*
14. There is no abyss	*57*
15. Healing on Hartwell	*58*
16. Zoom Out	*59*
17. Things that feel like Healing	*61*

Author's Note

There has always been a part of me that has never felt "enough". Not smart enough, not beautiful enough, not successful enough, thin enough, good enough, fill in the blank. This ever present "missing piece" left me feeling broken, I never felt complete.

For as long as I can remember I have struggled with my mental health. While I was not diagnosed with an eating disorder, major depression or OCD until I entered college, that "not enough" feeling coupled with a chemical imbalance and environmental triggers led me to months of mental health hospitalizations, experience in treatment programs, trying every medication combination possible and in thirteen years of (and ongoing) therapy.

Although this has been the hardest work of my life, it has also brought me so much! It has given me purpose, community, inspiration, something I am passionate about, the opportunity to become an entrepreneur, and the true ability to help people (all I have ever wanted) especially since creating Bake it Till You Make it LLC.

Bake it Till You Make it LLC is a community based organization that uses food and baking to cultivate authentic mental health conversation in the kitchen, around the table and beyond. While the mission of supporting others through storytelling has stayed consistent, the methods have evolved. What began as a compilation cookbook celebrating the resilient stories and favorite recipes of over forty individuals has become an additional series of four other books, workshops, presentations, events and media projects. Bake it Till You Make it has always been about the raw and the real but also the fun and joyous. I have worked to put mental health in terms that are non threatening...ones that are healing.

Over the years and through the series of Bake it Till You Make it books, I have explored all different kinds of recipes. From cake pops and breads to a wide variety of bakes contributed by others, I have used recipes as a way to connect with my readers and this book is no different.

In addition to a collection of poems chronicling all parts of my mental health recovery, you will also find recipes here. More specifically cookie recipes. To me, cookies are the ultimate reminder that we are not broken. Regardless of their irregular shape or texture, at the end of the day, they are still cookies. Whether I have burnt them, they crumble or stick to the pan, they are still delicious and valuable regardless.

I have often felt my mental health challenges have set me apart. My life's path has unfolded very differently than how I thought it would before my mental illness derailed my life. In some ways and on many days, I am grateful. My mental health challenges have brought me purpose, community, connection, clarity and endless opportunities but have also caused me pain, heartbreak and have at times threatened my life. And yet all parts of the journey are also parts of me.

As I challenge myself to embrace this: to value, to honor and to believe all of my experiences have only brought me closer to my truest self, I hope you do the same.

In the process of compiling these poems and recipes, I have had the opportunity to truly embody the idea that there is room for all parts of us. The crumbled pieces that we may want to brush aside, they are still valuable, they are still "us". You may feel lost. You may feel broken, but the truth is you have always been complete just by being you. Life breaks us down, it forces us to crumble at times, but it only strengthens who we are at our core— we always seem to heal.

Extending all of my beautiful, imperfect, heartfelt and crumbly love to you. Thank you for joining me on my poetic journey. This process has helped me grow, heal and accept. I can only hope it does the same for you. You are never alone and you have ALWAYS been complete.

With love and sprinkles on everything,

Dayna

Chapter One: Everything But The Kitchen Sink Cookie Recipe

Learning to embrace the painful, the messy, the beautiful and everything in between.

Ingredients

- 1 ½ cups all purpose flour
- 1 teaspoon baking soda
- ¼ teaspoon salt
- ½ cup unsalted butter
- ½ cup brown sugar
- ¼ cup granulated sugar
- 1 large egg
- 1 teaspoon vanilla extract
- 1 ½ cups chocolate chips
- 1 ½ cups peanut butter chips
- 1 cup mini marshmallows
- 1 cup toffee bits
- 1 ½ cups crushed pretzels

Directions

1. Preheat the oven to 350F.
2. In a bowl combine flour, baking soda and salt, set aside.
3. In a large bowl beat butter and both sugars.
4. Add egg and vanilla, beat until combined.
5. Slowly add the flour mixture, beating until combined.
6. Add in mix-ins, one cup at a time, and stir until combined.
7. Scoop 2 tablespoons worth of dough, roll into balls and place on a sheet.
8. Bake cookies for 10-12 minutes.
9. Let cool and enjoy.

The "S" Word

I used to cry when I was called "sensitive"
I believed sensitive was synonymous with weak
So much so
I believed sensitive people were not meant to withstand the weight of life
That being sensitive
Meant that you would break within moments of difficulty
Crushed by the boulders of challenge
Only compounded by the uncertainty of life
I believed
That the sensitive soul was fragile
Once it burst
It could never be repaired.
I didn't want to be sensitive,
I couldn't imagine my soul shattered
And yet I am sensitive!
Call me the "S" Word
And I will admittedly get emotional
But show me a challenge
And I will fight
Lay boulders on my shoulders
And I will dissolve them with my tears
I may be sensitive but
I am also
resourceful
Show me a soul that shimmers like mine does
It may have been shattered a few times
Under the guise of believing that being tough is strong
But I know the spirit
I have modge podged back together
Is brave.
I am strong
Because I am
Sensitive.

1am

My best ideas wake me up at night
My raw wish to inspire at 1am
Pummels the perfectionistic walls
I have built by day
There are
No rules at night
Just a free flow
And true sense
Of me
No inhibitions
Just truth

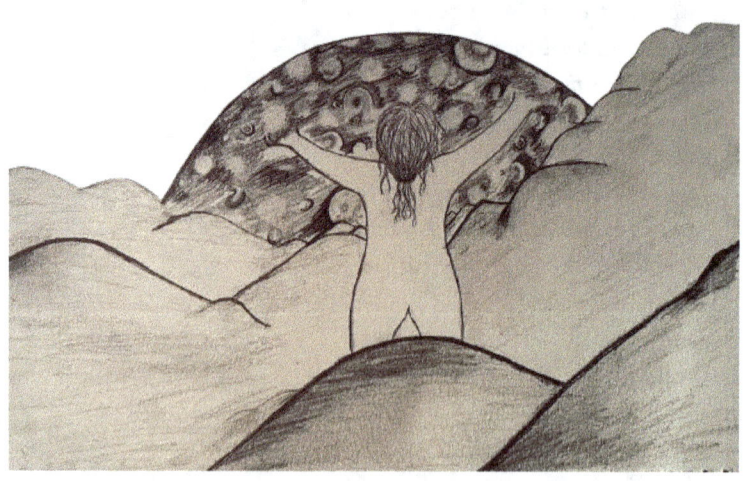

Limelight

Being on stage
Has always come easy
The bright lights that
Warm my body
Ignite a flame
In my soul
It continues to burn
Even when the lights
Go down
It feels good to be seen

Emetophobia

I didn't know you could become addicted to Tums
I guess when you are desperate for relief
You will try anything
The expensive supplements
The heating pad solutions
The panicked prayer
My emetophobia has trapped me
I wonder what I would think about
If I didn't have this paralyzing fear
Instructing my every choice
I am a puppet
Controlled by obsessions
And compulsions
I live attached to this demanding
String of intrusive thoughts
The overwhelming fear of vomit
Is habit at this point
Playing and replaying
Every scenario

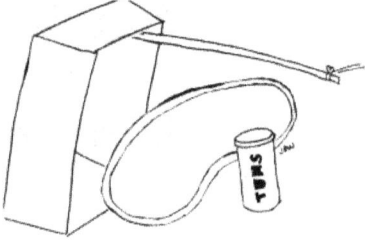

My old therapist said this fear lives within me Like the lyrics of my favorite childhood song
I can recite every word to the Spice Girls
"Wanna Be"
Without any effort
The lyrics flow seamlessly
Like
The emetophobic loop tapes play in my mind
An innate memorization of this pattern Emetophobia is woven into every part of my brain All I "wanna be"
Is free from this

Public Speaker

*My old therapist said
I picked the worst profession*

*For someone with OCD,
I guess this is just another area*

Where I complicate things.

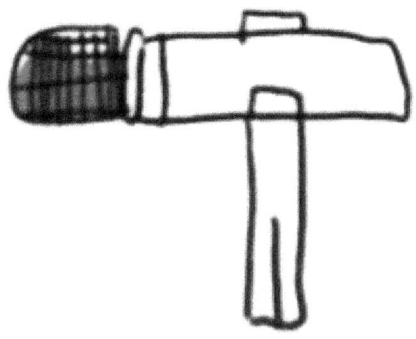

Depression is a heavy hitter
Too bad I was never any good at baseball.

Container

My therapist
Dena
Asked me to put
My pain in a container
A physical space for
My anguish
To live
Outside of my body
A place it can go
For awhile
To give me a break
From its intensity
She asked me to put my pain
On a shelf
And come back to it
When it feels safe
The pain lives in
An old water glass now
The one
I decorated with sharpie

Inside the jar there is
Fear
Disappointment
Heartbreak
Feelings I never thought
I could bear
But they are inside the jar now
And I am safe
I don't have to worry about a spill
I can be all of me
Without fear of an overflow
And yet I can still open the container whenever I need to
Or when I think I can,
But the pain sits outside of my body
Now
The feelings don't haunt me anymore

One

My brain operates in the world of
scarcity If I have one,
I am worthy I am loved
If she has one
Mine is gone,
She has taken it.
I am worthless
She is loved
I am scared
I am falling
Deep
Into a spiral of shame
If my heart believes in abundance
But my brain can't bear
To share
How can I operate with a mind
And heart
In opposition
How do I believe
That we can both have
One
We can both be worthy
How do I give to others
While also knowing that it will
Not take away
How do I know I am worthy
Because I am human
Rather than because
"I have one⋯"

Distraction

I fixed the aux cord in my car
So I can stop listening to myself think
I don't miss the noise
At all

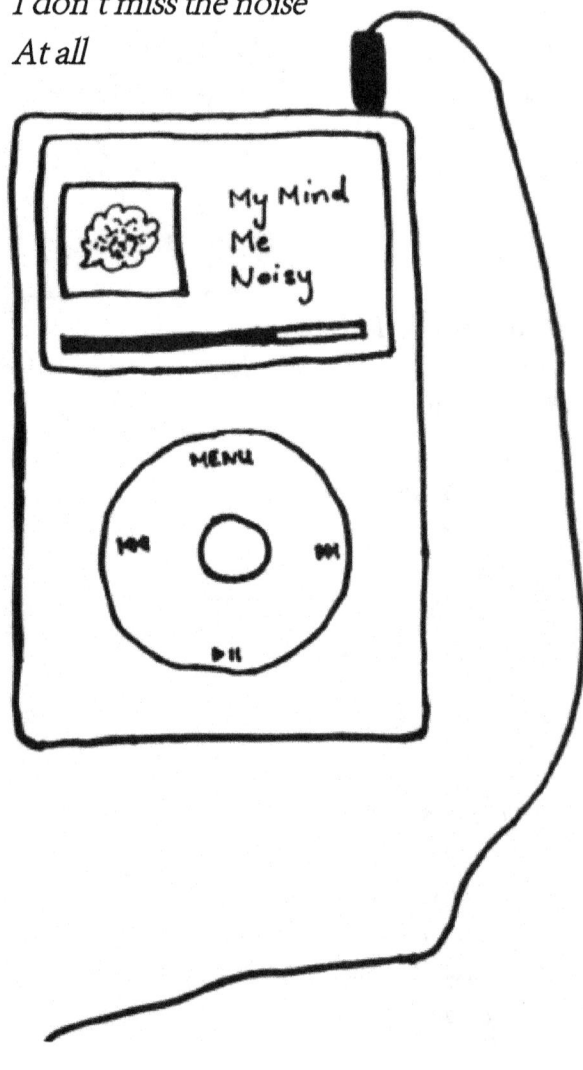

Rx

My new therapist
Kelly
Prescribed me
"Self-compassion"
If only this practice was as easy as
picking up my lexapro at Walgreens
Maybe it wouldn't feel so esoteric..

She says self-compassion is an inner offering
An acceptance
That we deserve the same respect
We give to others
If only it was that easy …

My mind is flooded with memories
Of younger me
Filling my middle school notebook margins
with scribbles that said: "I hate me"
I knew then like I know now
Those words would never leave my lips
If I was talking about anyone else
But
That's the thing
I can show compassion to anyone
Yet turn it inwards and I am stuck
It's not just those scribbled lines in my notebook from 15 years ago

These feelings are
Etched into my
Deepest wounds believing
I have to hate myself to be
Selfless
To be "good"
To be lovable
I actually don't think I hate myself
I think I just need to learn
How to live
With self-compassion

Social Anxiety

He asks me
"What are you so afraid of?
And I tell him
I actually have no idea⋯.

Friend?

The stories I make up in my head
About our "friendship"
Keep me company
When you don't call me back
I feel as lonely at 30
As I did at 13
It's hard to know which part of me
Shows up
When you don't get my call

Depression

What if I told you I don't actually know how to relax.
What if I told you I am scared to take that deep breath
I am always telling you to take.
What if I told you I don't know how to slow down.
What if I told you I don't know how to be me without this.
What if I told you sometimes it's hard to know me at all.

Joy

Words flow easier
When I am in pain
Poems seem to write themselves
I am on autopilot
I know how to operate
In the dark
Joy is different
Joy is new
Joy is light
Joy doesn't come with articulate
Paragraphs or words that come easy to me
Joy though
Is here to stay
So I better add some words to my vocabulary

Death Anxiety

It truly takes everything in me
To refrain from typing
"What happens when you die?"
Into the Google research bar
Knowing I can't truly know
Is why I'm anxious in the first place
Something I know is inevitable
And yet not "figure-it-out-able"
No wonder why I am scared.

Dominos

When one person
Stops pursuing what they love
The whole world stops
The inevitable impact of one life on another
When you stop showing up
There is a ripple
A drop in the ocean
Has a
Transcendent effect on the shore line
What you deem as washed up words
Are the sentiments that saved someone else
Seeing you try
And show up
Every day
Has kept me going
Even though you may not know it
You are the domino at the edge of the table
You stop
We all fall
What a beautiful burden to put on
One person
When you recognize your life
Can save another it stops feeling
Like a responsibility
But an honor
There is a reason
We don't give up on each other
We would all fall apart

Things That Feel Like a Hug:

1. When I see my name spelled correctly
2. When the cat that hates me purrs
3. When someone trusts me
4. When the restaurant server brings a pitcher of Diet Coke to the table
5. When I get to talk about Bake it Till You Make it
6. When I think about speaking at the White House
7. When a presentation audience member tells me their story
8. Pizza that has pineapple on it
9. Any Sunday night HBO TV show
10. Having a house guest
11. Listening to the We Can Do Hard Things podcast when I am stuck in traffic
12. Seeing a show on Broadway
13. Walking by the ocean with Noah Kahan in my headphones
14. My husband opening the front door when he hears me coming home
15. Writing a poem I know will resonate with someone
16. New products at Trader Joe's
17. Baking on a Sunday afternoon
18. Listening to Jazz music while I'm concentrating
19. Solving the Wordle in 3 tries (or less!!!)
20. Finding snail mail in my mailbox
21. When my therapists tell me they are proud of me
22. Buying coffee for the person behind me
23. Getting up and trying again

Chapter Two
The Complexities of Living in Diet Culture:
Sugar Cookie Recipe

"It ran in my family til it ran into me···"

Ingredients:

- ½ cup unsalted butter
- 1 cup granulated sugar
- 1 large egg
- 1 tablespoon vanilla
- 2 cups all purpose flour
- ¼ teaspoon baking soda
- ¼ teaspoon baking powder
- 1 teaspoon salt
- 1 cup sprinkles

Directions:

1. Preheat the oven to 350F.
2. In a bowl, cream together butter and sugar.
3. Add the egg and mix until well combined.
4. Add the vanilla and continue to stir.
5. In a separate bowl, whisk together flour, baking soda, baking powder and salt.
6. Add the dry ingredients to the wet ingredients to create a dough.
7. Portion out cookie dough into balls and roll in a small bowl filled with sprinkles to coat.
8. Place the dough balls on a baking sheet and chill for 30 minutes.
9. Once the dough is chilled, bake for 12 minutes.

Hunger

Every time I say
I'm hungry"
My inner child begins to weep
Knowing what comes after
Is disappointment
Is disgust
Hunger is a trigger
Needs are a trigger
Perfect girls don't need anything
They perform
They are quiet
They are certainly not hungry.
It hurts to know this is still hard to express
An innate knowing
I try to push away
All I have known is shame
When the gnawing in my stomach
Begins to pang
It is easier to just stay quiet

Perfect

As a perfectionist for the last 20 years
I know that when someone calls me perfect
I have lost all traces of myself
My opinions
My values
My voice
Perfection
Is in the eyes of the beholder
If you see me as perfect
I must be playing the part well
Saying the right things
Pleasing
Smiling
But strip down those layers and then what do you see?
If she doesn't smile
Or dress well, does she still suit you?
No amount of validation
Will ever leave me feeling perfect
I can play the part
But that doesn't mean
I don't feel
Empty

100 Things
I Would Rather Discuss Than Your Diet

1. Your passions
2. What you care about
3. Current events
4. The weather
5. Your family
6. Your friends
7. Life updates over the past week
8. Your favorite childhood recipe
9. What you think about growing older
10. Your favorite music
11. Your new favorite hobby
12. What you have loved since you were a kid that you still carry with you today
13. Your favorite recent purchase
14. The latest trend you have fallen in love with
15. What you do when you can't sleep
16. Your favorite TV show of all time
17. The movie that gives you the most comfort
18. A life hack you learned recently
19. What's on your Tik Tok FYP (For You Page)
20. How about them Red Sox
21. What sport you played in high school
22. What you are most excited about for your high school reunion
23. Your latest mistake
24. How your family is doing
25. Your favorite season
26. Your most treasured holiday tradition
27. The song you can't stop listening to
28. Your future plans
29. Predicting the outcome of your favorite sports team
30. Whether or not you have regrets
31. Your favorite quote
32. How you have come to believe in yourself
33. Your last sent text message
34. The last time you cried
35. Your future goals
36. Your favorite part of the year so far
37. Your most memorable travel experience
38. If you are a homebody or an adventurer
39. If you feel Taylor Swift saved the economy
40. If you are religious or spiritual

41. If you like to journal
42. Your dream pet
43. If you prefer dogs or cats
44. How you take your coffee
45. Your favorite pizza toppings
46. If you consider yourself lucky
47. If you believe everything happens for a reason
48. A seemingly small decision that changed the course of your life
49. If you believe that life is a simulation like the Sims computer game
50. Your favorite conspiracy theory
51. If you think it is easier to say goodbye or hold on
52. Your worst break up
53. How you handle the end of a friendship
54. The last brainstorm session you had
55. Your favorite mode of transposition
56. Your biggest fear
57. If you like the circus
58. If you prefer going to the movie theater or watching a movie in the comfort of your own home
59. Your current hyper fixation
60. If you are a Disney adult
61. Your favorite emoji
62. Something you feel embarrassed about
63. What you do when you are overwhelmed
64. Your favorite subject in school
65. How quickly you have fallen in love
66. What you think of the Bachelor franchise
67. The best Taylor Swift song
68. If you like country music
69. Your favorite radio station
70. How you pass time on a plane
71. Your favorite piece of art in your home
72. If you would ever join a recreational sports league
73. Your thoughts on the best Halloween candy
74. If you were to write a book what would it be called
75. How you handle anxiety
76. How many hours of sleep you get
77. If you like to cook or bake more or neither
78. If you like thunder and lightning
79. What your career would be if money was not an object
80. How you would design your personal heaven

81. How you would design your personal hell
82. How you liked your first job
83. How easy you feel customer service can be
84. Your credit score
85. Your favorite piece of technology
86. The invention you feel moved our society forward
87. If you feel social media is a blessing or a curse
88. How you handle being sick
89. What you hope for the next generation
90. If you fear public speaking or enjoy it
91. If you enjoy being the center of attention
92. Your favorite water bottle brand
93. If you believe in yourself
94. How hard you feel it is to start over
95. How you met your partner or how you think you will meet them
96. If you think online dating is helpful or hurtful
97. Who your favorite Kardashian is
98. If you enjoy following pop culture
99. If you like change
100. How you would design your future
101. Literally anything but your diet

Preoccupation

*I never worried about the size of my butt
Because you told me it was small once
You said my high school body was your dream
I never worried about my ass again.
I have worried about my stomach for too long
In seventh grade you pointed out
The "problem area"
And I have never let that go
When I look in the mirror
I see my stomach first
I always hate it.
I will always worry about you
The way you would rather
Die
Then eat a potato
It is still hard for me to understand
That you will always choose
Your eating disorder
Over your daughter
I know it's an illness
I know it's not actually you
But it's the only you I have ever known
And
I know she doesn't like my body.*

Dad's Dilemma

You say my poetry is a gift
That you can feel my warmth
As your eyes unwrap my words
I just don't know if you think that is enough.

Intersection

I am at the intersection of my dream
And the fear of its actualization
I crawl beneath the covers
And hide from reality
As I wonder
What it might actually mean if I know what I am doing.

I am at the intersection of recovery
And defeat
An assumption that you know how I feel about my body
By looking at it
I hear your words
As I shrink my body
In my largest sweatshirt

I am at the intersection of relaxation
And rumination
A day to myself to rest
Leaves me alone in my mind
And circling the depths of every thought that passes through it

I don't know if I am where I want to be
Or seven years old again
It feels one and the same

I am at the intersection of my life in this moment
And every moment after it
I want to control it all
To know it all
To see it all
But I also know I have no power in it
So I might as well try to let go
And live at this crossroads

Finally some relief...

*Tears stream freely down my face
They Hydrate the desert
Of my Sorrow*

Pedestal

I used to think that to love someone
You had to put them on a pedestal
Loving them
Looking to them
Above you
Praising the ground
They walk on
Because you are quite literally
Beneath their feet
Constantly
Plotting
Planning
How do I make them love me
From down here?
How can they see me
Under this platform
I have put them on,
I only really want to be loved
And accepted
And seen
Can they see me if I
Stand beside them?
I have heard
To love someone
You must share equally
But

*I am not sure how to ration
My emotional resources
Because these days my healing
Takes all of me,
I don't know how to share myself
When we are equals
And yet it is so easy
When you are above me
To let you know I can
See clearly
That your worth is so much more than mine
I used to believe
to believe that love
Was synonymous with idolize
When really I am learning
Real
Healthy
Honest love
Is to be shared
And you can't do that
From a pedestal*

Note to Self:

*If people don't respond to me,
I am not going to chase them.
If that means we are not friends anymore,
I will grieve them.
It will hurt
But I will move on
I always move on.*

Bride

Planning a wedding as a feminist with an eating disorder
Is as complicated as it sounds.
How do I honor something new
Without borrowing my old habits
How do I find a dress
Without being asked about my diet?
How can I frame "I am not changing my last name···"
In a way that you will hear
How is it that women have come this far in the world
Only to have their whole lives boiled down to one day
One promised to be the best of their existence
And then what are they?
Given away by one man
Only to be taken by another ***
Tell me,
What will you say
When you are asked about this day?
Will you tell them it was the beginning and the end
Or will you tell them
You have so much more to do
Will you tell them
You can be partnered
And independent
In love
And a free thinker
A wife
But also an artist

***we celebrate and value all love here but it just rhymed well

I guarantee
Your wedding dress was beautiful
But I bet the sparkle of your soul
Shimmers even brighter
Than the white sequin gown

A wedding
Is a day
Not a destination.
A woman is anything
And everything
She wants to be
Including
But not just a bride

Pain

He tells you he loves you
But you have no idea why
It's not like a list of qualities would help
You think he hates you
Because
You hate you
That hurts

34 Constitution

If I could wrap my arms around my childhood
My home would be at the center of that hug
The rooms filled with memories
The family gathered around the table
At holidays
The same stairs I took my first steps
I walked down for my junior prom
The doors I slammed in pain
Are the same ones that opened to opportunities
The house I took for granted
Will be someone else's soon
The halls that hold the memories
I will no longer get to walk down
The photos have been taken off the wall
The ones
That captured all of the life lived here
I will
Never have a house again like this one
This is where I will always call home

Up all Night

*Am I happy
or am I distracted?*

Things That Feel Like Heartbreak

1. Going to the Emergency Room
2. Any and every Lewis Capaldi or James Arthur song (I still love them though)
3. Dropping a piece of pottery
4. Loss of any kind and at any level
5. Breaking a glass
6. Seeing your parents cry
7. Letting someone or something you love go, because deep down you know it is for the best
8. Movies that are intentional tear jerkers
9. Longing for something familiar
10. Longing for something you never had
11. Disappointing someone you love
12. Failing a test
13. Not feeling good enough
14. Shame spirals
15. Heavy tears
16. Hate and every-ism we face as humans
17. The 2016 and 2024 elections
18. Being picked last in gym class
19. Painful texts read but not responded to
20. Emotional pain that no one else understands
21. Being judged
22. Let downs
23. Forgetting what it's like to believe in yourself

Chapter 3 A Rare Favorite:
Oatmeal Raisin Cookie Recipe

Vulnerability shouldn't have to be rare.
It is what connects us, it is what makes us human.

Ingredients

- 1 cup unsalted butter
- 1 cup brown sugar
 - ½ cup granulated sugar
- 2 large eggs
- 1 tablespoon vanilla
- 1 ½ cups flour
- 1 teaspoon baking soda
- 1 teaspoon cinnamon
- 1 teaspoon salt
- 3 cups oats
- 1 cup raisins

Directions

1. Preheat the oven to 350F.
2. In a bowl, cream together softened butter and both sugars until smooth.
3. Add in the eggs and vanilla, set aside.
4. In a separate bowl, whisk the flour, baking soda, cinnamon and salt.
5. Add the wet ingredients to dry.
6. Add in oats and raisins, the dough will be thick.
7. Chill the dough for 60 minutes in the fridge.
8. Line two large baking sheets with parchment paper.
9. Roll dough into balls and place 2 inches apart on a baking sheet.
10. Bake for 12 minutes and enjoy!

I Know

I know the ache
I know the way people say they understand
But they don't
I know how lonely it feels
Like you are the only one
That
Can't see what's ahead of them
I know the draw to the inspiring
The groups
The songs
The prayers
I know you hate this about yourself
I know how it feels to watch the world move on without you
I know how it feels when people tell you they love you
And you believe that's because they don't really know you
Or they don't know this part
The darkness
The depth
The hole inside that can never quite be ignored
I know what it's like to want to stay
But I also know what it's like to want to go
To believe there is something beyond this pain
I know how it feels
To be so full
Yet feel so empty

Transcranial Magnetic Stimulation

*TMS held the key
I didn't know existed
The one
That unlocked
The cell
I have lived in
Since I was 13
My depression
Became part of the jail
I was stuck in
I became comfortable on its
Cot
Subject to the darkness
And only what was necessary to survive
But now I can live In a bit more color
I didn't know the cloud that hung
Over this cage
Could ever break
Even just enough
For the light to shine through
I'm so glad it has*

Sabotage

The juxtaposition of
Wanting love
And the benefits of isolation
Has kept me trapped for too long
I want a partner
But that means
I would have to worry
Worry about the germs they track inside
Worry they will get sick or hurt or die
My brain likes to sabotage in that way
Singlehood protected me
From life's pain
But it also kept me
From love
Love I wanted more than anything
But that also means panic stricken nights
Of indescribable worry
If I love too deeply
What happens when it's gone

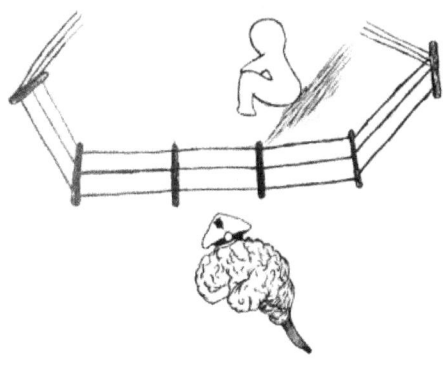

I Miss My Big Feelings

I miss the way I used to cry
Tears flowing freely down my face
No matter where I was
I miss the way my vision would blur
When I heard the melody of my favorite
Song
Because somehow weeping in the middle of a restaurant
Or in the produce aisle of the grocery store
Was what reminded me that I was human
I miss the depth of my empathy
The way I could insert myself
Into the shoes
Of a stranger
Feeling their anger
Walking in their pain
My soul used to boil with every injustice
Facing
Any adversity
It doesn't feel that deep anymore.
I miss the way I used to get excited
At the prospect of something new
My imagination
Drifting to every possibility
Now I see the reality
And I just feel numb
I miss my big feelings
Because I miss the way they
Made me feel alive.

I miss my tears
My values
My excitement for the future
I miss me
And I want her back
I look forward to
The day I feel myself again I
miss the beautiful anguish Of
my human experience
Because it is mine

This Life

The discrepancy between
The time I give those
Who deplete me
And the time I give myself
Is embarrassing (??)
Is harrowing (??)
Is disappointing...
To come this far on a path
Of self love only to
Turn around at the finish
Line
I have never given up easily
But somehow when the choice is
To walk one more mile alone
Or in the shoes of someone else
Their path looks more exciting
Whether it's curated
Or their true reality
When will my path
Be the one I pick
When will I feel that one is enough

...Enough
All I have ever wanted is to be enough
Enough of that want...
What I want
Is to not think about being enough
I want to know what it feels like to know
I am innately worthy
Of love
Not with a project in my head
Or a vegetable in my hand
What about what's in my heart
What does that count for?
I pause and whisper
"A lot"
As if the 8 year old girl who lives within me
Can hear that reply
Maybe if she knows I'm listening to her
She won't feel like she has to steer me
Down a path that isn't mine
Because in the end
This is the life I have been given
And in my heart I know
It is the life I would pick

Ghost

When I am depressed
I am a ghost at the dinner table
I wipe my tears on the sleeves
Of my sweatshirt
Hoping no one will see my eyes
Behind my glasses
I work to form
Words from the corners of my mouth
That maybe if I am talking about current events
I will forget about
The reality of my own
Yet,
I'm never really "there"
Only slightly less anxious when distracted
It's being present that is
Making these tears pool
Under my chin
I'm a ghost at the dinner table
Sometimes even sitting on a chair
Is hard

Too short

*I have never been able to
Reach for unconditional belief in myself
My arms have always
Fallen too short
To latch onto an undeniable
Sense of certainty and
Pride when it comes to
Believing in me.
Each time I practice and
Stretch my arms
To shorten the distance
Between my flexed
Finger tips
And what feels just slightly too scary
To grasp
I swing back and forth
On a tightrope
Between
My current reality
And what I could unleash
If I would just let myself
Hold on to what I have been racing toward*

*Maybe if I recognized
I would still have purpose
Without the chase,
I would have deemed myself
Worthy years ago.
Maybe then I could
Embrace what has
Always been
Just so slightly out of reach*

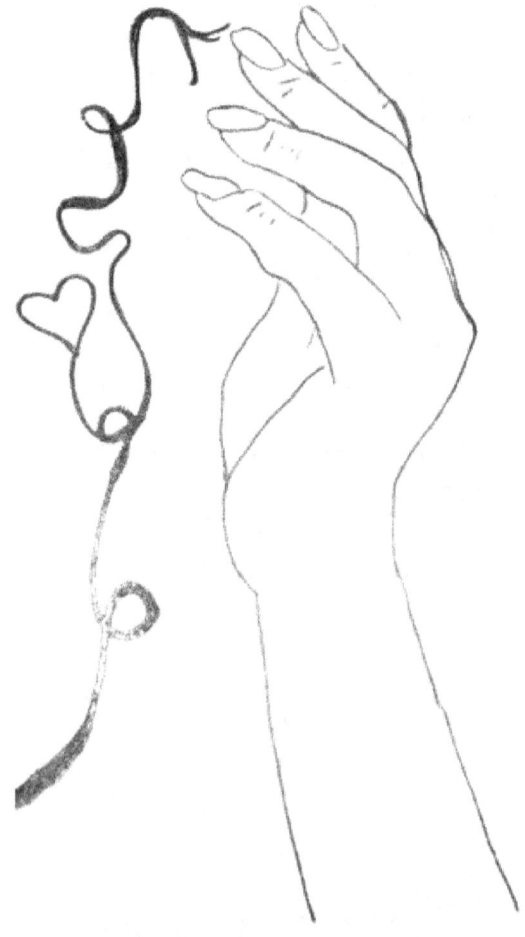

Present

We don't need a purpose to be alive
Existing is more than enough
It's our most precious gift.

Loved

If all I want to be is loved
Why is it so hard to accept?
It's so easy to give
It's all I want
Why can't I let it in?

Christmas Eve-Eve

Every December 23rd
For the last ten years
I have taken 1mg of klonopin
at bedtime
In hopes of experiencing
It's true tranquilizing
Effects
And yet every year
In the early hours of
Christmas Eve
Despite my best
Medicated efforts
I wake up
I usually wouldn't pay much attention
To the clock after midnight
But on this day
I already know what time it is
My body knows
Somehow the assault that took
Place five thousand miles away
At ten years of distance
Is right in front of me again.
I am transported from my twin
Bed in southwest Florida
To Jerusalem
I am watching myself
Become a victim again
Being subject to humiliation again
Being told I am overreacting again
Being told to be quiet

*But I can't keep quiet
I may have frozen ten years ago
But there is no statute of limitations
On finding your voice
And trusting yourself
That's a life long journey for me
One with a major
Detour that took
Place on
Christmas
Eve
The memories
The Reminders
They derail me
But taking my self seriously
Is my
Innate navigation system
The fastest way back to myself
Is to listen,
To hear,
To believe.*

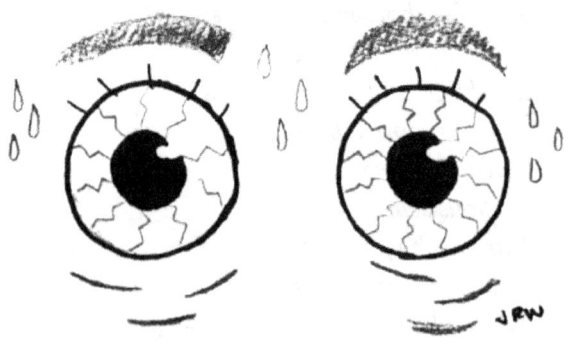

Stay

I look up at the ceiling of the store
And I am no longer 30 years old
It is not a sunny Friday in March
I am no longer at work
I am in my college bathroom
It is snowing
I am 19
Standing at the mirror
Looking up at the ceiling
Questioning what it would be like to die here
Knowing that I wouldn't find the answer in the ceiling
But maybe it would stop the crying
Maybe it would stop the thinking
Maybe it would stop the pain that
Comes with the complexity of
Being me
The unpredictable
Emotional
Seesaw
That seems to
Be the only way I can feel.
The paint has chipped at the
Fulcrum
A symptom
Of its overuse,
I am at its mercy
And yet none of this
Is new to me
Here I am
Again
Staring at the ceiling
Practically 11 years apart
Knowing so much has happened in between these moments
But I'm not sure how
I got back here.
How will I know if I want to live again?

Perfectionist

Will I always be a "work in progress"?
If so,
How will I know
When the work is over
Since I'm the one setting
The impossible
Expectations

The painful truth

The more successful I am
The more alone I feel.

There is no abyss

I stand on the edge
Of the unknown
One step too far
I could fall into the abyss
The no coming back
The drowning in grief
Forever
The too scary to face
I distract myself in every direction
To avoid this
The one step too far
I could fade
Swallowed whole
By the belief
I can't handle what I can't see
The only way out is through
But what if it means going through
The painful
The unthinkable
"How do you know there is not a net to catch you at the bottom"
My therapist
Dena
Asks
What if there is no abyss
What if taking a step off the edge pushes you
To a new place
A trampoline to
Spring you forward
What if there is no abyss
What if
There is someone to catch you at the bottom
And it's always been
You

Healing On Hartwell

It's not the absence of fear in here
It's the presence of courage
It's not a perfect recovery
It's a steady unraveling
A weekly choice
To dig deep within
To drudge up the messy
The ugly
The hidden
The feelings
That have no ending
The ones that know no bounds
They follow me everywhere
But in here we heal it
In here
We value it
We value honesty
We value truth
It is in here
I have identified my values again
It is in here I have reclaimed some of my power
It is in here I feel safe enough
To be brave

Zoom Out

*You feel like you are the center of the world
Every person
And Experience
Orbiting around you
Like the planets rotate
Around the sun
You feel like everyone hates you
And is mad at you
Or that somehow
Their bad mood is your fault
Their pain is your fault
You are the problem*

*You don't think of yourself as selfish
But you also believe people are thinking about you constantly
What you did wrong
Your annoyance
Your voice
You want to take up less space
You want to crawl under the covers for awhile
And move out of the way of the sun
A stark juxtaposition
To your fire
Sign energy
The fear of being seen
Only comes when you
Feel ashamed
But beautiful girl
Please zoom out*

Zoom out and see the world around you
Turn down the volume of the intrusive thoughts
And listen to the birds
Stop walking through fire
And place your feet on the grass
Or press them gently into the sand
Know you are amazing
And important
But no one is thinking about you
The way you think they are
We are all at the center of our own
Orbit
It's okay to zoom out
It's okay to know that you
Are just as important in the center of the universe
As you are behind a dark cloud
And
You don't control it all
Not other people
Not actions
Not even what happens in your life,
But you can
Zoom out

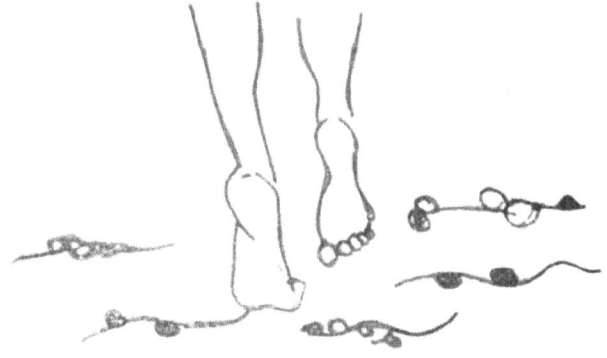

Things That Feel Like Healing

1. Breakthrough therapy sessions
2. Forgetting what depression 'feels like"
3. Finding jeans that you love and feel good, where you have completely disregarded the size
4. Expressing hard emotions to a trusted person
5. Being able to see practice pay off
6. Art of all kinds
7. "Thinking of you" texts just because
8. Showing up in the world the way you want to show up
9. Taylor Swift's discography
10. Facing the same difficult situation, but reacting differently
11. Poetry
12. Painting
13. Genuine laughter
14. Watching the sunrise on the beach the morning of my birthday
15. A glimmer on the pavement after an evening of summer rain
16. Completing a skincare routine when brushing your teeth a month ago felt impossible
17. Baking brownies when it snows
18. Ice cold water
19. Being outside
20. Having quiet time in your head that doesn't feel scary
21. Feeling relieved
22. Innately knowing you are loved
23. Happy tears
24. Feeling ready for what's next

About the Author

Dayna Altman is an energetic and dynamic mental health speaker, entrepreneur and advocate. The full force and sole operator of Bake it Till You Make it LLC, Dayna harvests her passion for mental health advocacy by using food and baking to create an authentic recipe for vulnerable storytelling.

The author of (now) five mental health cookbooks, the facilitator of a variety of mental health presentations and the subject of an award winning documentary, Dayna is a sought after storyteller. Dayna has been invited to speak at national conferences, in community kitchens, on the news and most notably, at the White House in 2022.

With experience working in both clinical and advocacy mental health settings, Dayna's breadth of knowledge in the field informs her work as does her own recovery.

Today, Dayna lives with major depressive disorder, obsessive compulsive disorder and is in lifelong eating disorder recovery.

When shes not testing out new recipes in her kitchen or quoting her therapists, Dayna is in pursuit of creating art as a means to explore new ways to change the world using her own story.

Illustration Credits

Dayna Altman
Public Speaker
Bride
Stay

Gabby Alvarez
Hunger
Pain
I Miss My Big Feelings

Mekkailah Chourb
Social Anxiety
Depression
I Know
Ghost
Zoom Out

Allee DeFronzo
One
34 Constitution Drive

Iwinosa Foster-Efosa
The S Word
1AM
Sabotage
The Abyss

Melody Gregory
Preoccupation
Pedestal
Present

Beth Hobbs
Distraction

Jason Taglieri
Friend?
Up All Night
The Painful Truth

Jenna Williams
Emetophobia
Depression is a Heavy Hitter
Dominos
Intersection
Finally Some Relief
TMS
Christmas Eve-Eve

Crumbled Not Broken: Embracing the Mess in Healing and Baking is a collection of poems and cookie recipes that celebrate the growth, acceptance, heartbreak and healing that comes with honoring all parts of ourselves we once felt were broken.

Created by mental health advocate and entrepreneur, Dayna Altman of Bake it Till You Make it LLC, *Crumbled Not Broken* covers topics of personal battles with depression, an eating disorder, living with OCD, emetophobia, surviving sexual violence, among others.

The poems in this book honor both the beautiful and the messy parts of mental health recovery as well as the journey to find one's voice in a world that so often leaves us quiet.

All poems have been illustrated by members of the Bake it Till You Make it community.

www.ingramcontent.com/pod-product-compliance
Lightning Source LLC
Chambersburg PA
CBHW072136070526
44585CB00016B/1707